Volcanoes on Earth

I0807846

Bobbie Kalman

Crabtree Publishing Company
www.crabtreebooks.com

Created by Bobbie Kalman

For my Aunt Blanka, with love.
You have always been an excellent role model!

Author and Editor-in-Chief
Bobbie Kalman

Research
Molly Aloian

Editor
Robin Johnson

Photo research
Bobbie Kalman
Crystal Sikkens

Design
Katherine Berti
Samantha Crabtree (cover)

Production coordinator
Katherine Berti

Illustrations
Jim Chernishenko: page 26
Robert MacGregor: page 6
Dan Pressman: page 7

Photographs
© Dreamstime.com: page 19 (bottom)
© iStockphoto.com: pages 1 (except background), 8, 9 (left), 12 (top), 13 (middle right)
© 2008 Jupiterimages Corporation: page 17 (top)
© Shutterstock.com: cover, pages 3, 4, 5, 9 (top right), 11 (bottom), 13 (except middle right), 14 (top), 15, 16, 17 (bottom), 18, 19 (middle), 20, 21, 22-23, 24, 25, 26, 27 (except inset), 28 (top), 29, 31
Wikimedia Commons: page 27 (inset)
Other images by Corel and Digital Stock

Library and Archives Canada Cataloguing in Publication

Kalman, Bobbie, 1947-
Volcanoes on earth / Bobbie Kalman.

(Looking at earth)
Includes index.
ISBN 978-0-7787-3205-1 (bound).--ISBN 978-0-7787-3215-0 (pbk.)

1. Volcanoes--Juvenile literature. I. Title. II. Series.

QE521.3.K34 2008 j551.21 C2008-900926-6

Library of Congress Cataloging-in-Publication Data

Kalman, Bobbie.
Volcanoes on earth / Bobbie Kalman.
p. cm. -- (Looking at earth)
Includes index.
ISBN-13: 978-0-7787-3205-1 (rlb)
ISBN-10: 0-7787-3205-3 (rlb)
ISBN-13: 978-0-7787-3215-0 (pb)
ISBN-10: 0-7787-3215-0 (pb)
1. Volcanoes--Juvenile literature. I. Title. II. Series.

QE521.3.K35 2008
551.21--dc22

2008004845

Crabtree Publishing Company

Printed in the U.S.A./112015/SN20150910

www.crabtreebooks.com 1-800-387-7650
Copyright © **2008 CRABTREE PUBLISHING COMPANY**. All rights reserved. No part of this publication may be reproduced, stored in a retrieval system or be transmitted in any form or by any means, electronic, mechanical, photocopying, recording, or otherwise, without the prior written permission of Crabtree Publishing Company. In Canada: We acknowledge the financial support of the Government of Canada through the Canada Book Fund for our publishing activities.

Published in Canada
Crabtree Publishing
616 Welland Ave.
St. Catharines, Ontario
L2M 5V6

Published in the United States
Crabtree Publishing
PMB 59051
350 Fifth Avenue, 59th Floor
New York, New York 10118

Published in the United Kingdom
Crabtree Publishing
Maritime House
Basin Road North, Hove
BN41 1WR

Published in Australia
Crabtree Publishing
3 Charles Street
Coburg North
VIC, 3058

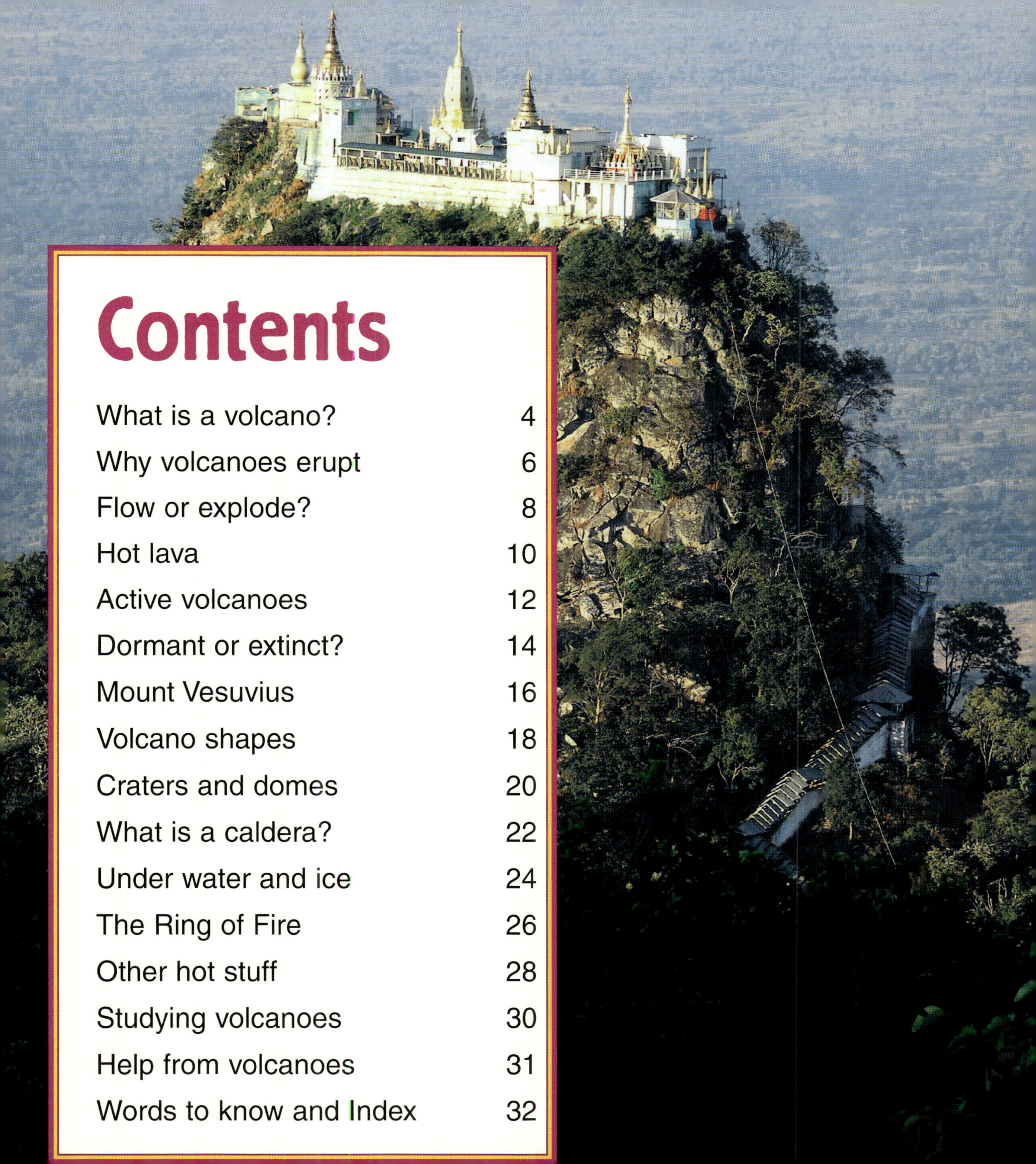

Contents

What is a volcano?

A **volcano** is an opening on the Earth's surface. Volcanoes can **erupt**. When volcanoes erupt, **lava**, rocks, and dust burst out of them. Lava is hot melted rock. The volcano in this picture is erupting.

Mount Rainier is a volcano in Washington State. It last erupted in 1854.

A volcano is also a mountain

The word "volcano" is also used to describe a **mountain** that has formed from a volcano. A mountain is a very high, steep area of rocky land. Volcanoes can make tall mountains. The mountain in this picture is Mount Rainier. This high mountain has **glaciers** on it. Glaciers are slow-moving rivers of ice.

Why volcanoes erupt

Earth is made up of four main layers. Two layers are in the **core**, or the center of Earth. These layers are called the inner core and the outer core. Above the core is a layer called the **mantle**. The mantle contains **magma**. Magma is very hot melted rock. The top layer of Earth is called the **crust**. We live on Earth's crust. Volcanoes erupt when heat and **gases** build up under the crust and need to come out. They burst out through volcanoes.

Earth's layers

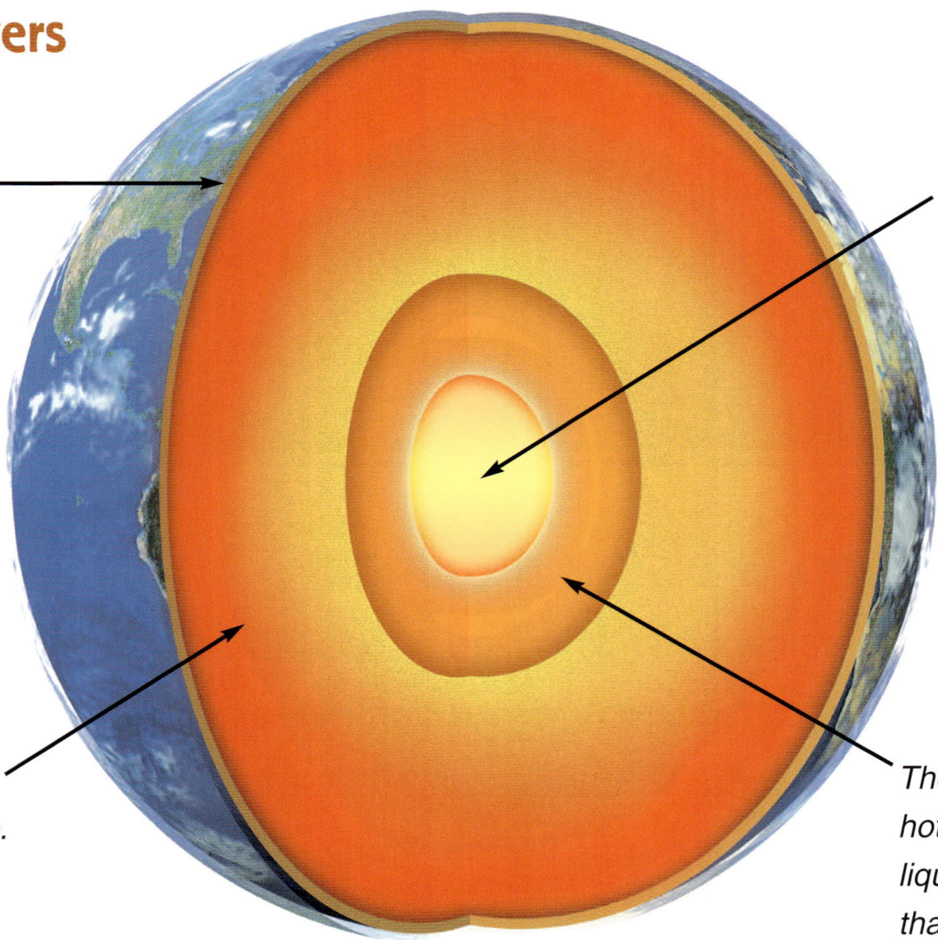

We live on Earth's crust.

*The inner core is **solid** metal. A solid is something with a firm shape.*

Magma comes from the mantle. The mantle is under the crust.

*The outer core is hot **liquid** metal. A liquid is something that flows freely.*

Look inside a volcano

This picture shows the inside of a volcano. Gas, **steam**, dust, **ash**, lava, and rocks are flying out of the **vent**. The vent is the top of a long opening. Some volcanoes have several vents. The smaller vents are on the sides of the volcanoes.

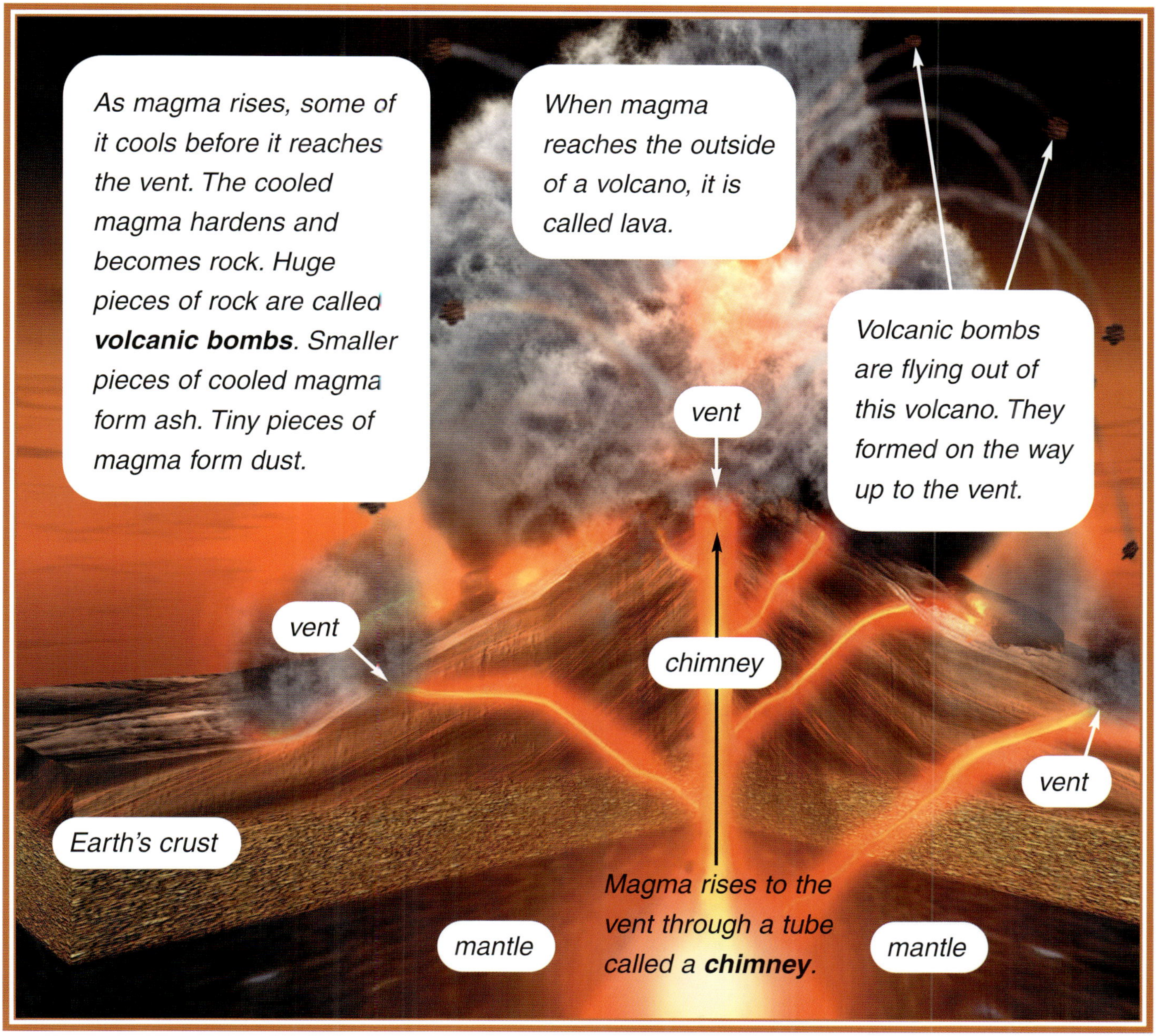

Flow or explode?

Volcanoes erupt in different ways. Some **eruptions** are quiet. Lava flows down the sides of the volcanoes. Other eruptions are like explosions. They shoot lava, ash, and volcanic bombs high into the air. Some eruptions last for only a few seconds, whereas others last for many years.

Lava, rocks, and ash are exploding out of this volcano.

Dangerous eruptions

Some eruptions are not dangerous. A large eruption, however, can be very dangerous for people who live near the volcano. There is nothing that people can do to stop most eruptions. They can only get out of the way!

The hot lava from these volcanoes has burned trees and roads in its path.

Hot lava

There are different kinds of lava. Some lava is thin. Thin lava flows down the sides of volcanoes very quickly. It can flow hundreds of miles or kilometers before it cools and turns into rock. Thin lava often turns into smooth, hard rock. A skin forms on the surface of the lava.

This thin lava has formed a skin on its surface.

Thin lava has flowed quickly down the sides of this volcano. The lava will turn into rock in the cool ocean.

Thick, slow lava

Other lava is thick and sticky. It explodes out of vents and moves slowly down the sides of volcanoes. Thick lava does not move very far. It cools and piles up to make rocks. The large rocks in the picture below were formed from thick lava.

*This volcano in Northern Ireland erupted millions of years ago. When its thick lava cooled, the lava shrank and cracked. The cracks formed thousands of **pillars**, or tall rocks.*

Active volcanoes

An **active** volcano is one that has erupted recently or one that might erupt at any time. There are more than 1,500 active volcanoes on Earth. A few of Earth's active volcanoes are shown on these pages.

Mauna Loa and Mauna Kea are two volcanoes in Hawaii. Mauna Loa is the biggest active volcano on Earth. Its last eruption was in 1984. Mauna Kea is no longer active.

*Kilauea is an active volcano in Hawaii. A steady stream of lava flows from Kilauea into the ocean. The lava cools, hardens, and forms new land. The **islands** of Hawaii were all created from lava.*

Will they erupt?

Some active volcanoes do not erupt for many years, and then they suddenly erupt again. Other active volcanoes erupt every day. Many volcanoes that erupt every day are not dangerous to people.

Mount Etna is a volcano in Italy. It has been erupting for more than 3,500 years, but it is not dangerous.

Arenal Volcano in Costa Rica has erupted every day since 1968. Before then, it was not active.

Furnace Peak is a very active volcano on Reunion Island. It shoots out a lot of lava.

Mount St. Helens in Washington State had a huge eruption in 1980. More than 50 people were killed, and many homes and bridges were destroyed. Railways and highways were also ruined.

Dormant or extinct?

A **dormant** volcano is one that has not erupted for many years but might become active again. A volcano that is **extinct** has not erupted for thousands of years. Mount Fuji is a volcano in Japan. It has not erupted for 3,000 years. Is Mount Fuji a dormant or an extinct volcano?

Mount Kilimanjaro in Tanzania, Africa, has not erupted since people have lived on Earth. Gas comes out of its sides, however, and scientists think it could erupt again. What do you think?

The eruption that formed Diamond Head in Hawaii was probably short and happened only once. Scientists think it will never happen again. Is Diamond Head dormant, or is it extinct?

People live at the top of this extinct volcano. Many others climb up to have a look.

Mount Popa is an extinct volcano in Myanmar. Many trees and other plants grow in the area around Mount Popa. Plants grow well in soil that is part volcanic ash.

Mount Vesuvius

Mount Vesuvius is a famous volcano in Italy. It erupted almost 2,000 years ago, destroying the cities of Pompeii and Herculaneum. Thousands of people died when they were buried under ash and mud.

Many people travel to Italy to see the ***ruins*** *of Pompeii. Both pictures show the ruins. This picture also shows Mount Vesuvius.*

Is it still active?

Vesuvius has erupted many times. In 1631, more than 3,000 people died, and villages were buried under lava. In 1906, the volcano shot out a huge amount of lava, killing many people. There have been no eruptions since 1944, but people who study volcanoes think that Vesuvius may erupt again. Is Vesuvius active or dormant? People who live nearby hope it is dormant!

When Vesuvius erupted in 1906, people grabbed whatever they could carry and ran for their lives.

Vesuvius is thought to be a very dangerous volcano because millions of people live near it. They live in the city of Naples, shown above, and in areas around the city.

Volcano shapes

Volcanoes come in different shapes. Some volcanoes have flat tops. Some volcanoes look like **mounds**, or short hills. Other volcanoes look like cones. Cone-shaped volcanoes with steep sides are called **cinder cones**. When cinder cones erupt, **cinders** and lava fall down the sides of the volcanoes. Cinders are small pieces of rock and ash. The cinders and lava build up after each eruption. They create the steep sides of the volcanoes.

These cinder cone volcanoes formed on the side of Mauna Kea volcano in Hawaii.

Most volcanoes are **stratovolcanoes**. Stratovolcanoes are tall and cone-shaped. They are made up of many layers of hardened lava and volcanic ash. Stratovolcanoes have big, explosive eruptions. The lava that flows from them is thick. Stratovolcanoes are also called **composite volcanoes**.

Mount Fuji is a stratovolcano.

Mount Shasta is a stratovolcano in California.

Shield volcanoes are the largest volcanoes on Earth. Their sides are not steep. The lava from shield volcanoes flows slowly across the ground.

Mauna Loa is a shield volcano.

Craters and domes

Many volcanoes have **craters**. Volcanic craters are round, bowl-shaped openings at the tops of volcanoes. They form around the vents of volcanoes. Some craters are large and deep. Some are filled with water. The crater in this picture is called Monti Silvestri. It is part of Mount Etna volcano in Italy.

Dangerous domes

Lava domes are often found in the craters of active stratovolcanoes. Lava domes are made of very thick, slow-flowing lava. The lava does not go far. It builds up into mounds near the tops or sides of the volcanoes. Lava domes are very dangerous volcanoes! They often erupt with huge explosions.

This volcano's crater is filled with water.

What is a caldera?

A **caldera** is a large circular hole in a volcano. It is not the same as a crater. A caldera forms after a large eruption has caused a lot of magma to pour out of a volcano. Without enough magma to hold up the mountain above it, the center of the volcano **collapses**, or falls inward. When the volcano collapses, it creates a huge hole. The hole may be several miles or kilometers wide.

Wizard Island is a volcano that formed in a caldera.

Deep lakes in calderas

Over time, calderas fill with rainwater and turn into lakes. There is a deep, wide lake in Oregon that formed in a caldera. The lake is called Crater Lake. Although the lake's name has the word "crater" in it, the lake is not in a crater. It is in a caldera.

Crater Lake is the deepest lake in the United States.

Under water and ice

When a volcano erupts in an ocean, lava spills onto the bottom of the ocean. The lava cools and becomes hard. With each eruption, the lava piles up and the volcano grows taller. After many eruptions, the volcano rises above the surface of the water and forms an island.

The Galapagos Islands are volcanic islands.

The Hawaiian Islands are also volcanic islands. Big Island in Hawaii is still forming. This picture shows a black-sand beach on the island. The sand was made from cooled lava and ash. The rocks around the beach were also made from cooled lava.

Breaking the ice

Some volcanoes form under thick glaciers. When some of these volcanoes erupt through ice, **tuyas** are formed. Tuyas are volcanoes with flat tops and steep sides. They are found throughout Iceland, Antarctica, Oregon, and British Columbia, Canada. Ring Mountain, shown below, is a tuya in British Columbia.

The Ring of Fire

There are volcanoes on every **continent**, but more than half of Earth's volcanoes are in the Pacific Ocean. They are found in an area called the Pacific Ring of Fire. Parts of Asia, North America, South America, and Australia and Oceania are in the Ring of Fire. Indonesia, which has 130 active volcanoes, is in this area. The map below shows this dangerous area of Earth.

These volcanoes are in Java, Indonesia.

The pink area shows the Ring of Fire. The small red triangles are volcanoes.

The volcanoes named here are not all active.

Krakatau (Krakatoa)

Krakatau is an island in Indonesia. It is also the name of the island's volcano. Krakatau has erupted many times. The most famous eruption was in 1883. It was the worst volcanic eruption in modern times. The eruption killed thousands of people and destroyed many nearby towns. It also destroyed two-thirds of the island of Krakatau.

Krakatau today

Krakatau before 1883

Kamchatka Peninsula

The Kamchatka Peninsula in Russia is among the most active volcanic areas along the Pacific Ring of Fire. There are over 100 volcanoes in Kamchatka, and more than a dozen are active. Tolbachik, shown below, is an active volcano. It is made up of two volcanoes. One is a flat-topped shield volcano, and the other is a cone-shaped stratovolcano.

shield volcano

stratovolcano

Other hot stuff

Hot springs are streams of heated water that come up from the ground. They are found where there is volcanic activity under the Earth's crust. There are hot springs all over Earth, even in oceans. A **geyser** is a type of hot spring that erupts regularly, throwing hot water and steam into the air.

Yellowstone National Park has many hot springs and geysers. This geyser is called Old Faithful. It erupts ***faithfully****, or loyally, about once every hour.*

The Grand Prismatic Spring in Yellowstone National Park is the largest hot spring in North America. The water in the hot spring is clear and clean.

The Valley of Geysers in Kamchatka has more than 90 geysers. This picture shows some of the geysers and ***fumaroles****. Fumaroles are openings in the Earth's crust that let out gases and steam.*

These macaque monkeys are in a hot spring in Nagano, Japan. It is winter, and snow is falling on their heads. The monkeys are not cold, however. They are having a nice hot bath!

Studying volcanoes

*This volcano **observatory** keeps an eye on volcanoes.*

Volcanology is the study of volcanoes. People who study volcanoes are called **volcanologists**. Volcanologists **observe**, or watch carefully, the world's volcanoes. They look for cracks in the Earth. They measure changes in the shapes of volcanoes and in the movements deep inside Earth. By studying volcanoes, volcanologists can help **predict** future eruptions.

These people are visiting a volcano and learning about it from a volcanologist.

Help from volcanoes

Volcanoes can cause a lot of damage, but they are also very helpful to the Earth and to people. Volcanoes can provide clean heat. They also fill the soil with **minerals** that help plants grow.

Clean heat

In Hawaii, New Zealand, and Iceland, there are hot rocks under the Earth's crust. The rocks heat water that is under the ground. The heated water gives off steam. The steam is used to make **energy**. This kind of energy is very clean. It does not dirty the land or water. The heated water is also pumped into people's homes.

These pipes are carrying heated water into homes in Iceland.

New plants

After a volcano erupts, the dust and ash make the soil around the volcano very **fertile**. Plants that have died grow back quickly, and they are healthier than ever before. This beautiful plant is growing in soil that was covered in lava and ash.

Words to know

Note: Some boldfaced words are defined where they appear in the book.

caldera A large circular hole that is made when a volcano collapses on itself

continent One of the seven huge areas of land on Earth

crater The large opening at the top of a volcano; smaller than a caldera

crust The layer of hard rock that surrounds Earth

energy The power to work or do things

eruption The release of lava, rocks, and other substances from a volcano

faithfully Happening as expected

fertile Describing soil in which many plants grow easily

gas A substance like air that is not solid or liquid, and which can move freely

glacier A large, slow-moving body of ice

island Land that is completely surrounded by water

lava dome A rounded, steep-sided mound built by eruptions of thick lava

magma Melted rock inside Earth that turns to lava outside a volcano

mineral A non-living substance found in nature that helps plants and animals grow

observatory A building with a telescope and other equipment, used to watch volcanoes

predict To tell something before it happens

ruins Parts of buildings that remain after a city has been destroyed

steam The gas that water turns into when it gets very hot

volcanic Relating to, or made by, a volcano

Index